Mola Ocean Sunfish

by Grace Hansen

Abdo
SUPER SPECIES
Kids

Abdo Kids Jumbo is an Imprint of Abdo Kids
abdopublishing.com

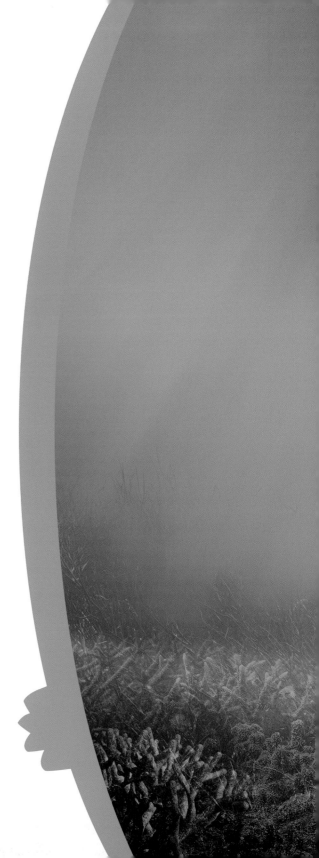

abdopublishing.com

Published by Abdo Kids, a division of ABDO, P.O. Box 398166, Minneapolis, Minnesota 55439.
Copyright © 2019 by Abdo Consulting Group, Inc. International copyrights reserved in all countries.
No part of this book may be reproduced in any form without written permission from the publisher.
Abdo Kids Jumbo™ is a trademark and logo of Abdo Kids.

052018

092018

Photo Credits: Alamy, Glow Images, iStock, Seapics.com, Shutterstock

Production Contributors: Teddy Borth, Jennie Forsberg, Grace Hansen

Design Contributors: Dorothy Toth, Laura Mitchell

Library of Congress Control Number: 2017960566

Publisher's Cataloging-in-Publication Data

Names: Hansen, Grace, author.

Title: Mola ocean sunfish / by Grace Hansen.

Description: Minneapolis, Minnesota : Abdo Kids, 2019. | Series: Super species |
    Includes glossary, index and online resources (page 24).

Identifiers: ISBN 9781532108242 (lib.bdg.) | ISBN 9781532109225 (ebook) |
    ISBN 9781532109713 (Read-to-me ebook)

Subjects: LCSH: Ocean sunfish--Mola Mola--Juvenile literature. | Body size--Juvenile literature. |
    Animals--Size--Juvenile literature. | Animal behavior--Juvenile literature.

Classification: DDC 597.64--dc23

Table of Contents

Mammoth Mola 4

Shark or Sunfish? 18

Food 20

More Facts 22

Glossary 23

Index 24

Abdo Kids Code 24

Mammoth Mola

Ocean sunfish are the heaviest **bony fish**.

Ocean sunfish live throughout the world's oceans. They are often found in warm waters near **coasts**.

The ocean sunfish's scientific name is *Mola mola*. *Mola* is **Latin** for "**millstone**." The fish got this name for its rock-shaped body.

If an ocean sunfish were a rock,

it would be a boulder. It is huge!

10

11

Ocean sunfish can weigh up to 5,000 pounds (2,268 kg). That is more than the weight of two great white sharks!

Ocean sunfish can grow up to 14 feet (4.3 m) tall. That is taller than a professional basketball hoop!

They can grow up to

10 feet (3 m) long. That is

longer than most dolphins.

Shark or Sunfish?

Ocean sunfish have huge **dorsal fins**. People often mistake them for sharks.

18

19

Food

These giant fish have small mouths. But they still manage to eat a lot! Jellyfish are their favorite food.

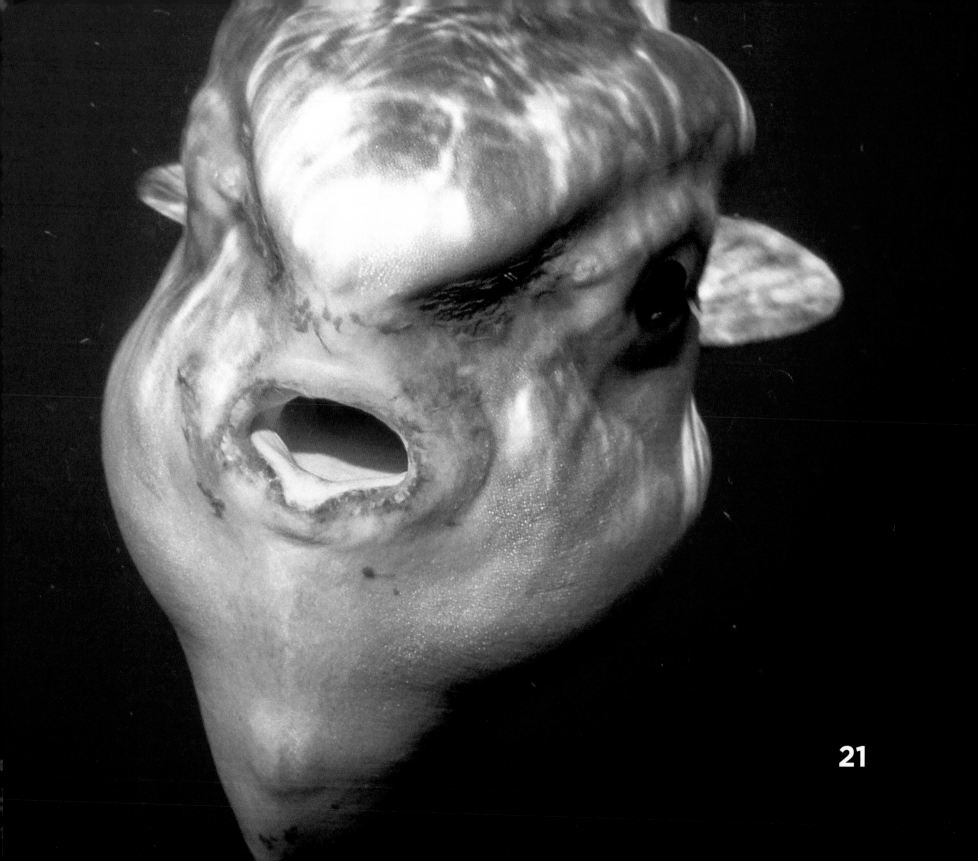

21

More Facts

- Ocean sunfish are just one-tenth of an inch (2.54 mm) long at birth.

- An adult ocean sunfish is 60 million times heavier than it was at birth.

- Ocean sunfish are not good swimmers. Their back fin, called a clavus, never grows.

Glossary

bony fish – a fish that has a skeleton made of bone.

coast – land near the ocean.

dorsal fin – a fin on the back of a fish.

Latin – the language of ancient Rome.

millstone – either of a pair of circular stones that grind something.

Index

fins 18

food 20

habitat 6

height 14

Latin 8

length 16

mouth 20

name 8

ocean 6

weight 4, 12

Abdo Kids
ONLINE
FREE! ONLINE MULTIMEDIA RESOURCES

Visit abdokids.com and use this code to access crafts, games, videos, and more!

Abdo Kids Code:
SMK8242